A WONDERFUL WORLD OF WEATHER

First published in 2018 by Wayland
Copyright © Wayland 2018

Wayland
Carmelite House
50 Victoria Embankment
London EC4Y 0DZ

Managing editor: Victoria Brooker
Creative design: Paul Cherrill

ISBN: 978 1 5263 0540 4

Printed in China

FSC
www.fsc.org

MIX
Paper from
responsible sources
FSC® C104740

Wayland is a division of
Hachette Children's Books,
an Hachette UK company.

www.hachette.co.uk

A WONDERFUL WORLD OF WEATHER

Written by
Kay Barnham

Illustrated by
Maddie Frost

WAYLAND

Did you know that there is a layer of air around our planet? This layer is called the atmosphere. It protects us from the Sun's rays.

When sunlight warms the atmosphere, air swirls
around the world. It is this movement of air that
makes all of our wonderful weather happen.

Today, the weather is sunny.
There are no clouds. There is no rain.
The wind is very light. The sun shines
brightly in a clear, blue sky.

Sunny days often happen in summer,
when the temperature is hot.
But they can happen in
winter too, when it might
be frosty and cold.

Look at these fluffy clouds. As they move
across the sky, the clouds hide the sun.
Without the sun's warmth, it becomes cooler.

Clouds form when the sun warms the ocean.
Water vapour rises into the air. As it cools, it
changes into tiny droplets of water and ice.
This is what clouds are made of.

Inside the dark clouds, the water droplets have grown bigger. They are now too heavy to stay in the air.

Splish, splash!
Plip plop!

Raindrops fall
back to Earth.
It's time to
put up the
umbrella!

When the weather is colder, ice crystals form inside clouds. These stick together to make snowflakes. When they become big and heavy, the snowflakes begin to fall.

Every snowflake has six sides.
Every single snowflake is different.

Sometimes, it is too cold for rain and not cold enough for snow. Sleet is a mixture of rain and snow. It starts to melt as it falls to Earth.

Hailstones are lumps of ice that form in thunderclouds. Some are tiny. Some are bigger than table tennis balls!

Thunderclouds are large,
dark and menacing.
Rain, hail, thunder
and lightning all come
from thunderclouds.

When ice particles inside
thunderclouds bash together,
lightning happens. It flashes from
cloud to cloud. Lightning also leaps
down to the ground. Thunder is the
sound lightning makes.

Frost only appears after cloudless clear nights,
when the temperature drops below 0ºC.
This is when water freezes.
Frost is frozen water vapour.

This spider's web is decorated with sparkly, twinkly frost. Meanwhile, the puddle of water has frozen hard. Watch out! The ice is very slippy.

Mist happens when cloud is so low that it touches the ground. When the cloud is very thick, it is called fog. It is very difficult to see.

Everyone must take great care when the weather is foggy. Cars travel slowly. Sometimes aeroplanes do not fly.

The sun warms some parts of Earth's atmosphere more than others. When air is warm, it rises. Meanwhile, cool air sinks. Wind happens because air moves around.

There are different strengths of wind. Sometimes,
it is light and breezy. Sometimes, it is very strong.
Sometimes, the wind blows so hard that it's hard to walk!

A hurricane is an enormous storm. The wind is so strong that it can damage houses and blow down trees. Sometimes, a hurricane makes the sea wash over the land. This causes flooding.

Did you know that hurricanes, typhoons and cyclones are all the same thing? The storm has different names in different parts of the world.

A tornado is a spinning column
of air. It sometimes happens when there is
a thunderstorm. The wind is so strong that it can
pick up buildings, trees, cars and animals.

A waterspout is a tornado
that forms over the sea.

When sunshine hits raindrops, the sun's light is split into different colours. A rainbow of red, orange, yellow, green, blue, indigo and violet light arcs across the sky.

Watch out for double rainbows. These happen when the sunlight is scattered twice by each raindrop!

THINGS TO DO

1. How many different types of weather can you fit into one painting? Look at the beautiful illustrations in this book for ideas.

2. Make a weather game. Instead of Snakes and Ladders, why not call it Sunshine and Showers? When a player lands on sunshine, move forward three spaces. When they land on showers, move back three spaces. Players roll dice to move their counters around the board.

3. Create a word cloud about the weather! Write 'WEATHER' in the middle of the page. Then add all the words this makes you think of. Write them all down using different coloured pens. Start like this...

RAINBOW

CLOUD WEATHER

NOTES FOR PARENTS AND TEACHERS

This series aims to encourage children to look at and wonder about different aspects of the world in which they live. Here are more specific ideas for getting more out of this book:

1. Encourage children to keep a weather diary. What sort of weather is happening today? Record the information by drawing a weather symbol for each day.

2. Use homemade or real musical instruments to make weather noises. The top notes on a piano might sound like tinkling rain. A drum made from a shoebox could sound like noisy thunder. Be as imaginative as possible!

4. Make a rain gauge using an empty plastic water bottle. Cut the top off for children and then ask them to mark measurements up the side of the bottle. Now put the bottle outside and wait for a downpour!

WEATHER BOOKS TO SHARE

Everything Weather
by Kathy Furgang
(National Geographic Kids, 2012)

Fact Cat: Weather
by Izzi Howell
(Wayland, 2018)

How the Weather Works
by Christiane Dorion,
and illustrated by Beverley Young
(Templar, 2011)

The Wild Weather Book (Going Wild)
by Fiona Danks and Jo Schofield
(Frances Lincoln, 2013)

Weather (*Usborne Beginners*)
by Catriona Clarke
(Usborne, 2006)

READ ALL THE BOOKS IN THIS SERIES:

A Stroll Through The Seasons
ISBN: 978 0 7502 9959 6

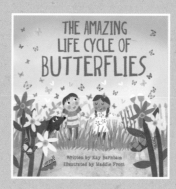

The Amazing Life Cycle Of Butterflies
ISBN: 978 0 7502 9955 8

A Wonderful World Of Weather
ISBN: 978 1 5263 0540 4

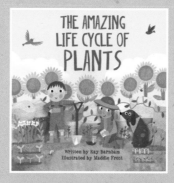

The Amazing Life Cycle Of Plants
ISBN: 978 0 7502 9957 2

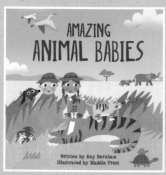

Amazing Animal Babies
ISBN: 978 1 5263 0592 3

The Awesome Night Sky
ISBN: 978 1 5263 0594 7

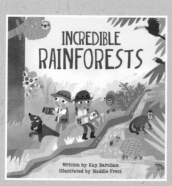

Incredible Rainforests
ISBN: 978 1 5263 0590 9

The Great Big Water Cycle Adventure
ISBN: 978 0 7502 9951 0